CHUCK NORRIS

CANNOT BE STOPPED

ALSO BY IAN SPECTOR

The Truth About Chuck Norris

Chuck Norris vs. Mr. T

400 All-New Facts about the Man Who Knows Neither Fear Nor Mercy

Ian Spector

CHUCK NORRIS

CANNOT BE STOPPED

GOTHAM
BOOKS

GOTHAM BOOKS
Published by Penguin Group (USA) Inc.
375 Hudson Street, New York, New York 10014, U.S.A.
Penguin Group (Canada), 90 Eglinton Avenue East, Suite 700, Toronto, Ontario M4P 2Y3, Canada (a division of Pearson Penguin Canada Inc.); Penguin Books Ltd, 80 Strand, London WC2R 0RL, England; Penguin Ireland, 25 St Stephen's Green, Dublin 2, Ireland (a division of Penguin Books Ltd); Penguin Group (Australia), 250 Camberwell Road, Camberwell, Victoria 3124, Australia (a division of Pearson Australia Group Pty Ltd); Penguin Books India Pvt Ltd, 11 Community Centre, Panchsheel Park, New Delhi – 110 017, India; Penguin Group (NZ), 67 Apollo Drive, Rosedale, North Shore 0632, New Zealand (a division of Pearson New Zealand Ltd); Penguin Books (South Africa) (Pty) Ltd, 24 Sturdee Avenue, Rosebank, Johannesburg 2196, South Africa

Penguin Books Ltd, Registered Offices: 80 Strand, London WC2R 0RL, England

Published by Gotham Books, a member of Penguin Group (USA) Inc.

First printing, May 2010

10 9 8 7 6 5 4 3 2 1

LIBRARY OF CONGRESS CATALOGING-IN-PUBLICATION DATA
Spector, Ian.
Chuck Norris cannot be stopped : 400 all-new facts about the man who knows neither fear nor mercy / Ian Spector.
p. cm.
ISBN 978-1-59240-555-8 (pbk.)
1. American wit and humor. 2. Norris, Chuck, 1940—Humor. 3. Norris, Chuck, 1940—Miscellanea. I. Title.
PN6165.S678 2010
796.8092—dc22
2010005042

Printed in the United States of America

Set in Monkton Book · Designed by Sabrina Bowers

TO THE READER:

Thanks for paying my rent;
keep up the great work!

Now that I've had the opportunity to write a third book, I've realized that most readers will most likely still just skip right over the boring few pages of introductory text and get straight to the goodies that lie within. This left me with a bit of a problem. Should I treat the reader to some witty anecdotes or fascinating true stories? While I would ordinarily jump at the opportunity, I realized that this time around, so little has happened in my life as it relates to all this that it would be as great a waste for me to write as it would be for you to read. Consider it a benefit; I get to make my submission deadline and you get to move on with your day faster than expected. Congratulations, you're already a winner.

Chuck Norris has the heart of a child. **HE KEEPS IT IN A SMALL BOX.**

When Chuck Norris gets pulled over, he lets the cop off with a warning.

Chuck Norris plays Battleship with the U.S. Navy.

When Chuck Norris tells time, time obeys.

Chuck Norris can tell which way a train traveled by looking at the tracks.

The truth will set you free. Chuck Norris will set you on fire.

Chuck Norris composed the soundtrack to "2 Girls 1 Cup."

Jaws made his last cinematic appearance in 1987. Coincidentally, Chuck Norris developed a liking for sushi in 1987.

Life comes at you fast. Chuck Norris's fist comes at you faster.

Some people see the glass half full, others see the glass as half empty. Chuck Norris always sees Scotch.

As a poor college student, Chuck Norris went to the local sperm bank to make some quick cash. He retired later that day.

ALL of Chuck Norris's genes are dominant.

Chuck Norris is just like Spider-Man, only instead of being bit by a radioactive spider, Chuck was bitten by a radioactive god.

Chuck Norris can play Russian roulette with a **FULLY LOADED REVOLVER** and win.

All eleven secret herbs and spices used in KFC can be found naturally in Chuck Norris's beard.

Chuck Norris once got a girl pregnant after phone sex.

With an accurate kick to the neck, Chuck Norris can turn any fruit into a vegetable.

People don't actually die of "natural causes." It's just something doctors use because there's only so many times you can say "Chuck Norris did it again" in one day.

The French surrender to Chuck Norris every day at 2 P.M.

Giraffes were created after Chuck Norris uppercutted a horse.

Leading hand sanitizers claim they can kill 99.9 percent of germs. Chuck Norris can kill 100 percent of whatever the fuck he wants.

Some kids piss their name in the snow. Chuck Norris can piss his name into concrete.

Chuck Norris doesn't cheat death. He wins fair and square.

Chuck Norris once won a game of Connect Four in three moves.

Chuck Norris doesn't have hair on his testicles because hair does not grow on steel.

The best part of waking up is not Folgers in your cup, but knowing that Chuck Norris didn't kill you in your sleep.

Chuck Norris eats the core of an apple first.

Chuck Norris once defeated a steam train in a jousting tournament.

Champions are the breakfast of Chuck Norris.

Chuck Norris became one-fourth Cherokee after winning the 1999 "Who Can Eat a Jeep?" competition.

Jack was nimble, Jack was quick, but Jack still couldn't dodge Chuck Norris's roundhouse kick.

When God said, "Let there be light," Chuck Norris replied, "Say please."

Chuck Norris can tie his shoes with his feet.

Most men are okay with their wives fantasizing about Chuck Norris during sex because they are doing the same thing.

Chuck Norris jizzes lightning bolts.

The city of Dallas was brought to a standstill after they renamed their main thoroughfare Chuck Norris Boulevard. Residents were terrified to cross Chuck Norris.

Chuck Norris can watch a season of *24* in just three hours.

Chuck Norris's family wraps his gifts in lead so he can't see what's inside.

Chuck Norris can set ants on fire with a magnifying glass—at night.

If at first you don't succeed, **YOU OBVIOUSLY AREN'T CHUCK NORRIS.**

There's strong. Then there's Army Strong. *Then* there's Chuck Norris strong.

When international spies are given a "license to kill," they are simply handed a picture of Chuck Norris.

If a tree falls in the forest and nobody is around to hear it, not only does Chuck Norris hear it, he probably had something to do with it.

My wife and I decided to name our son Chuck Norris. My wife is still in a coma, and I am learning to walk again.

Meat Loaf would do anything for Chuck Norris.

The only thing that gets between Chuck Norris and justice is an equal sign.

When dining out, Chuck Norris writes thoughtful and practical advice in the area on the bill marked "Tip."

Chuck Norris has been to Mars. That's why there's no life there.

In his will, Chuck Norris has specified that *if* he dies, he will bury himself.

Chuck Norris takes steroids, but only so that his balls will fit in his pants.

To raise their standards of safety, automakers now crash test their cars by paying Chuck Norris to run into them.

Chuck Norris's orgasm is the number one cause of drowning among women between the ages of eighteen and thirty-five.

Chuck Norris's Rice Krispies don't say shit until he gives them the OK.

Kellogg's
10 ESSENTIAL VITAMINS & MINERALS
FAT FREE!
RICE KRISPIES
TOASTED RICE CEREAL
Nutrition Facts

Chuck Norris had to give up drinking when gas went over three dollars a gallon.

Chuck Norris can break-dance on thin ice.

Chuck Norris was offered a part on the TV show *Heroes,* but he left after he found out it wasn't a documentary.

When Chuck Norris drinks, he never throws up.
HE ONLY THROWS DOWN.

Chuck Norris can create enough wind power with one roundhouse kick to power Sri Lanka for forty days.

Chuck Norris's roundhouse kick is an optical illusion. His right foot doesn't swing around and hit your head, his left foot spins the earth so that your head hits his foot.

Chuck Norris still doesn't know that *Walker, Texas Ranger* is just a TV show.

For six years, Chuck Norris was the FBI's chief negotiator. His job involved calling up criminals and saying, "This is Chuck Norris."

When Chuck Norris wants popcorn, he exhales on Nebraska.

After the deaths of ten child actors, the producers of *Sidekicks* finally decided to cut the scene where Chuck Norris pats the kid on the back for winning the tournament.

Chuck Norris once pulled a building out of a burning building.

When a reporter asked Chuck about his the decision to shave his beard, Chuck replied, "If I told you, I'd have to kill you." He then laughed a little bit, realizing that he was going to kill the reporter anyway.

Chuck Norris can do a handstand with both hands tied behind his back.

In baseball, a player is said to have executed a Chuck Norris when he scores ten or more runs in a single at bat.

Chuck Norris owns a custom belt sander with three settings: Low, High, and Shave.

Chuck Norris's computer has a live mouse attached to it.

Chuck Norris once hit the lottery. It was pronounced dead at the scene.

Fire escapes were invented to protect fire from Chuck Norris.

"High tide" and "low tide" actually refer to the times when Chuck Norris gets in and out of the ocean.

Chuck Norris went to the DMV and the clerk asked him for three forms of ID. He gave her a roundhouse kick, a whisker from his beard, and a *Walker, Texas Ranger* DVD.

A woman who once gave Chuck Norris a blow job died of tetanus.

Chuck Norris's morning run is along the Autobahn.

Chuck Norris doesn't have a CTRL key on his keyboard because Chuck Norris is always in control.

Chuck Norris describes his politics as "somewhere to the right of Hitler."

On his birthday, Chuck Norris randomly selects one lucky child to be thrown into the sun.

Chuck Norris was once charged with three counts of attempted murder in Colorado, but the charges were dropped because Chuck Norris does not "attempt" murder.

Consumer Reports, in their 2010 ranking of toilet papers, found Chuck Norris Texas TP to be the least effective brand on the market. It really is true that Chuck Norris won't take shit from anyone.

Chuck Norris irons his shirts while he's still wearing them.

Chuck Norris is such a good salesman that he once talked an Amish housewife into buying a plug-in dildo.

Chuck Norris once beat an orphan to death **WITH THE BODY OF ANOTHER ORPHAN.**

Chuck Norris keeps the undefeated 1972 Miami Dolphins in a large tank in his backyard.

Chuck Norris shot up heroin for eleven months just to prove how easy it was for him to quit.

A priest, a rabbi, and a minister walk into a bar. Chuck Norris roundhouse kicks them all in the face because he already knows the joke isn't going to be funny enough.

Chuck Norris has a closet full of exploding pants.

There are only weapons of mass destruction in Iraq when Chuck Norris visits.

Roosters crow in the morning to warn everyone that Chuck Norris is now awake.

Chuck Norris puts all his eggs in one basket and then stomps on the basket. Chuck Norris will not spend his time worrying about eggs.

In the movie *Titanic,* Chuck Norris has a brief cameo as "The Iceberg" in hopes of making the movie end sooner.

Chuck Norris invented the speed bump in 1958 when he left several corpses on a residential street and forgot to bury them in his flower garden.

Socrates was put to death after he posed the following philosophical puzzle to Chuck Norris: "Why did you sleep with my wife?"

Chuck Norris can make an entire bag of microwave popcorn just by slipping it down his pants.

While his vision may be compromised at night, Chuck Norris always has perfect death perception.

Chuck Norris goes Easter egg hunting with a loaded shotgun.

Chuck Norris can squeeze apple juice out of a banana.

Chuck Norris doesn't have an open-door policy but he does have a closed-fist policy.

Windows Vista runs just fine on Chuck Norris's computer.

In 1968 Chuck Norris went on summer holiday to London. He walked into a pub in St. John's Wood and promptly drank a full keg of Guinness. When the bartender asked him to pay his tab, Chuck Norris produced an enormous belch that lasted for ninety-three minutes and thirty-three seconds. Tape recorders running in a nearby recording studio captured this magical event and today we know this recording as the Beatles' *The White Album*.

God actually needed ten days to create the world but Chuck Norris only gave him seven because he *really* wanted to try out a sweet jump on his new bike.

Chuck Norris penned "If You're Happy and You Know it, Clap Your Hands" as a way to find victims.

The reason we haven't found Osama bin Laden is because Chuck Norris found him first.

Jesus could walk on water, but Chuck Norris can swim through land.

Chuck Norris won the 1993 International Jump Rope Championship standing completely still.

A sequel to *300* is currently being filmed starring Chuck Norris. It will be called *1*.

Chuck Norris once gave himself a lethal injection of potassium chloride to see if it would give him a buzz.

Conan O'Brien once installed a lever next to his desk that, when pulled, played a clip from *Walker, Texas Ranger.* In response, Chuck Norris installed a lever next to his desk that, when pulled, played footage of Chuck Norris having sex with Conan O'Brien's wife.

One time a third grader tried to impress Chuck Norris by burping the alphabet. In turn Chuck belched the entire *Gangs of New York* screenplay.

Hulk Hogan cried when he found out that his daughter Brooke had lost her virginity, but was really psyched when he found out that it was to Chuck Norris.

Chuck Norris's barber uses a blowtorch and the jaws of life to trim his beard.

Chuck Norris was invited to play a game of capture the flag and won after taking over all of Europe.

Once a year, the National Undertaker's Union holds a party in honor of Chuck Norris.

Chuck Norris is planning to open up a chain of retail stores called "Bloodbath and Beyond."

Chuck Norris shot his age at Pebble Beach when he was seventeen.

Chuck Norris won the Daytona 500 on the black dirt bike from *Delta Force*.

The fatalities in *Mortal Kombat* are actually re-creations of eyewitness accounts of Chuck Norris going apeshit during a traffic jam.

Unsolved Mysteries was really a documentary about Chuck Norris's greatest accomplishments.

Merriam-Webster prints a custom dictionary for Chuck Norris that doesn't have the word "remorse" in it.

When life gives Chuck Norris lemons, he makes orange juice.

Unlike Santa, Chuck never has to check his list twice.

The average human sperm has a 1 in 600 chance of becoming a human. Chuck Norris's sperm has a 1 in 10 chance of being wanted for murder in four states.

Chuck Norris actually picks his watches based on how many atmospheres it can withstand.

Chuck Norris has a $17 million life insurance policy out on his shadow.

Chuck Norris is the reason that Jack is in a box.

Chuck Norris routinely crushes cans on his forehead.
GARBAGE CANS.

Chuck Norris defeated an entire basement of Korean teenagers in *Starcraft.*

MILK
If Chuck Norris ever tells you he "feels like Mexican tonight," don't be surprised if you happen to find him screwing your housekeeper later that evening.

LIVE
VIDEO
LIVE
RIGHT NOW
NORRIS: TRYING TO CREATE
ONE WORLD ORDER
LUPITA

When playing poker with Chuck Norris, you might have the better hand, but he always has the better fist.

Chuck Norris was named after himself.

When Chuck Norris breaks the law, the law doesn't heal.

When working with Chuck Norris, common occupational hazards include crippling joint pain and death.

Chuck Norris doesn't lose weight; he discards it intentionally.

The difference between Chuck Norris and God is that Chuck Norris does not think he's God.

Bigfoot owns a grainy video of Chuck Norris.

Nocturnal animals just can't sleep knowing Chuck Norris lurks about.

Chuck Norris once broke a mirror on a black cat under a ladder on Friday the thirteenth and then won the lottery.

Chuck Norris tweaked his Harley to give it four-wheel drive.

Chuck Norris doesn't use toothpicks; he punches himself in the teeth until the chunks of food run for their lives.

Objects in Chuck Norris's rearview mirror are closer to death than they appear.

Chuck Norris was born with cowboy boots on. The spurs on his boots made sure that he wouldn't have a younger brother to compete with.

Dr Pepper is Chuck Norris's personal physician.

Chuck Norris once hit a deer with his car. He then promptly put the car back on the ground and continued driving.

Chuck Norris was banned from the Olympics after he won every gold medal and melted them down to make what he called "the perfect condom."

Chuck Norris makes plans to break plans.

The greatest trick the devil ever pulled was convincing the world that Chuck Norris was just an actor.

Chuck Norris is, therefore I am afraid.

Chuck Norris has brought a whole new meaning to the phrase "dressed to kill."

For Texas-issued driver's licenses, there are three choices under the "Do you choose to be an organ donor?" category: "Yes," "No," or "I am Chuck Norris and I will be providing the medical community with thousands of organ donors."

Chuck Norris plays ping-pong with an ironing board and a watermelon.

Chuck Norris whistles in German.

Chuck Norris fought and won a battle at the Red Sea, which was originally called the Blue Sea.

Chuck Norris can rub his stomach, pat his head, and perform an oil change at the same time.

Chuck Norris makes his internal organs pay rent.

In 1992, Chuck Norris passed a very large kidney stone. It currently sits atop his desk, making an excellent paperweight and a hell of a good conversation piece.

Chuck Norris plays Minesweeper with real mines and Hearts with real hearts.

METRO CITY PUBLIC
STOP

Chuck Norris once saved a busload of children from certain peril by watching them burn to certain death.

Chuck Norris would use guns if they didn't kill people so slowly.

King Kong built the wall around Skull Island to protect himself from Chuck Norris.

Chuck Norris was kicked out of the Army for never carrying a weapon into battle.

Not only can Chuck Norris throw his voice, he is lethal with it for up to two hundred yards.

The real secret to the success of *Girls Gone Wild* is that **CHUCK NORRIS IS THE CAMERAMAN.**

Chuck Norris plans to rid the world of hunger by killing the hungry.

Chuck Norris is the best thing before, after, and during sliced bread.

During a game of golf, Chuck Norris shot two holes in one, struck out nine batters, caught a three-hundred-yard pass, recorded a hat trick, and broke the single lap speed record at Daytona Speedway.

Chuck Norris employs a stunt double for his crying scenes.

The video game *Katamari Damacy* was inspired by Chuck Norris's tendency to roll Japanese families into balls and hurl them into space.

Chuck Norris smokes only the finest Cuban cigar rollers.

Chuck Norris doesn't need tickets to the gun show because he is the main event.

In the '80s, Chuck Norris marketed a children's cereal called "Chux." It did not sell very well due to the fact that it was made entirely of human teeth.

Chuck Norris's pickup does thirty miles per gallon of blood.

Chuck Norris is the only celebrity to have a death row named after him.

Jawbreakers were originally in the shape of Chuck Norris's fist.

Chuck Norris did not have childhood heroes, only competition.

Chuck Norris never has to pay a prostitute for sex, partly because they are so excited that they refuse to charge him, but mostly because he kills them.

When they say "it's raining cats and dogs," Chuck Norris is probably just visiting the local animal hospital.

A man once broke every bone in his body to avoid Chuck Norris doing it for him.

Parker Brothers created a special edition of Monopoly just for Chuck Norris. In his set, all of the Community Chest and Chance cards award him first place in a beauty contest.

Chuck Norris can do push-ups with both arms tied behind his back.

Chuck Norris knows more than ten thousand ways to molest a panda.

If Chuck Norris were a *Star Trek* character, he would be the ship.

Chuck Norris may not be able to turn water into wine, but he can turn Corona into urine.

Chuck Norris has a guesthouse made entirely out of Joan Rivers's vagina.

When ghosts go camping, they sit around the fire and tell stories about Chuck Norris.

Keanu Reeves studied acting under Chuck Norris.

Chuck Norris fights stains with the power of Tide.

Chuck Norris invented the hammer when he was tired of using his forehead to slam nails into wood.

Kill one man and you are a murderer; kill millions and you are a conqueror; kill them all and you are Chuck Norris.

Before Leo Tolstoy met Chuck Norris, his book was called *Peace.*

Chuck Norris struck gold while picking his nose.

ALL of Chuck Norris's toes are big toes.

When Chuck Norris puts his ear to a seashell, he always hears Mozart's Piano Concerto No. 27 in B Flat Major.

Chuck Norris currently owns the single largest collection of mummified cats in the world. When questioned about the motivation for such a collection, his only reply was, "They aren't ripe yet."

Doctors once found sixty dollars worth of nickels in Chuck Norris's stomach.

Chuck Norris has a hand-tooled leather vest made from the hide of a studio executive who displeased him.

Chuck Norris covers his Slip 'n Slide with gravel.

Chuck Norris is the official airline of the Cincinnati Reds.

When Chuck Norris orders a Bloody Mary, he expects to be given a woman named Mary, who he then beats to a bloody pulp.

Chuck Norris once stayed up all night playing poker with tarot cards. He got a full house and eight people died.

If you visit Chuck Norris's house, you can buy a shirt that says, "I fellated Chuck Norris and all I got was this lousy shirt and a mouth full of radioactive semen."

All the Yes album covers are Norris family photos.

Chuck Norris once had a cobra that he named Beverly. He taught it how to fetch and dial a phone. But then one day, it bit the maid. So with tears in his eyes, Chuck had to shoot the maid.

Everything Chuck Norris knows about kangaroos is false.

The phrase "rule of thumb" is derived from an old English law that stated that Chuck Norris couldn't beat your wife with anything smaller than his thumb.

Chuck Norris's blood pressure is measured in volts per kilogram.

Chuck Norris has the directions to Sesame Street in his GPS but refuses to tell anyone.

When Alexander Graham Bell made the first phone call, all he heard on the other end was Chuck Norris's heavy breathing.

Chuck Norris is the only survivor of the *Hindenburg*, the *Titanic*, and New Coke.

The only thing that could give Chuck Norris indigestion would be swallowing his pride.

The original title for *Alien vs. Predator* was *Alien and Predator vs. Chuck Norris.* The film was canceled shortly after going into preproduction. No one would pay nine dollars to see a movie fourteen seconds long.

Chuck Norris was the first man to successfully jump the island of Oahu in a Ford Taurus.

Chuck Norris owns all of the No. 1 pencils.

Chuck Norris is neither pro-choice nor pro-life. He is pro-death.

Chuck Norris is the reason why Cap'n Crunch was turned down for his promotion to admiral.

In the time it took you to read this sentence, Chuck Norris destroyed four thousand acres of rainforest.

If you play Pink Floyd's *The Dark Side of the Moon* and watch *The Wizard of Oz* without sound at the same time, Chuck Norris will beat you senseless for wasting your time.

Chuck Norris will concede that Gary Busey roundly defeated him in a tequila shot-for-shot competition, though Chuck notes that he had spent that morning inventing the printed word.

Chuck Norris once got into screaming contest with a horse.

Chuck Norris owns three dogs, two horses, and Regis Philbin.

Chuck Norris not only walks to the beat of his own drummer, he dances to the spin of his own dreidel and eats to the tune of Bon Jovi.

Chuck Norris owns the other half of the mask from *The Phantom of the Opera.*

Chuck Norris broke the record for the highest cannonball when he jumped from the International Space Station into the Indian Ocean.

The only type of fever Chuck Norris ever gets is disco fever.

Chuck Norris once punched a hole in a cow just to see what was coming up the road.

Chuck Norris tightrope walked across the Pacific Ocean, stopping only once, in Guam, to liberate it from the Spanish.

The concept of a geocentric solar system makes Chuck Norris sexually excited.

Chuck Norris can tell when a woman is ovulating just by sticking his fist down her throat.

When visiting Hawaii, Chuck Norris always makes sure to have unprotected sex with a volcano.

Chuck Norris's rap sheet actually rhymes.

Chuck Norris's idea of a balanced diet is a forty-eight-ounce steak in each hand.

The real reason Hitler killed himself was because he found out Chuck Norris was Jewish.

Chuck Norris puts the "fun" in "funeral."

Before you die, you see the ring on Chuck Norris's right hand.

ALL of Chuck Norris's teeth are wisdom teeth.

Chuck Norris keeps his balls in a holster and his dick in a guitar case.

Chuck Norris's turds float so well that one of them won the gold medal in the two-hundred-meter backstroke at the 1984 Olympics.

The movie *Congo* was filmed entirely in Chuck Norris's crotch.

Chuck Norris doesn't have to cut his grass; he just stands on his porch and dares it to grow.

Chuck Norris is diversifying into pharmaceuticals. He will soon be releasing two new products. The first is a medication to help control hemorrhoids. It is called "Preparation—Chuck's Foot." The other product is used to control erectile dysfunction. It is called "Chuck's Other Foot."

The credit crunch is part of Chuck Norris's morning workout.

Chuck likes his meat so rare that **HE ONLY EATS UNICORNS.**

Most children remember bringing an apple to school for the teacher. Chuck Norris brought the teacher's ex-husband's heart in a plastic baggie.

Chuck Norris once climbed Mount Everest by accident.

The word "fuck" is in fact a portmanteau of "foot of Chuck."

Chuck Norris hates ballerinas because they twirl all day and not a single person gets roundhouse-kicked in the face.

Not only is he part of the Mile High Club, Chuck Norris is also in the Mile Long Club and the Mile Wide Club.

Chuck Norris has a tattoo above his pelvis that reads, "Tastes great, more filling!"

All of the actions performed by a Chuck Norris action figure are hate crimes.

Chuck Norris wants to allow prayer in school, but only prayers to him.

Every night before going to sleep, the bogeyman checks under his bed for Chuck Norris.

Chuck Norris can stare you down with his back turned.

Chuck Norris has been scientifically proven to be cheaper and more effective at preventing premature aging than the world's leading beauty products. For just twenty dollars, Chuck Norris will agree to show up unannounced at your house at some point just before your thirtieth birthday and kill you.

All of Chuck Norris's formal attire is made of denim.

The last time Chuck Norris woke up after a night of binge drinking, he found himself negotiating the terms of the Louisiana Purchase.

If Chuck Norris takes out a loan, the only collateral he provides is collateral damage.

Chuck Norris's favorite pickup line is made of one-eighth-inch steel cable, has a tensile strength of 4,700 pounds, and is tied at one end to a Ford Bronco.

Chuck Norris can make a horse cry just by dropping his pants.

When Chuck Norris has a crush on a girl, it usually ends with a few broken bones.

When Chuck Norris threw a frat party in college, it was out of a third-floor plate-glass window.

Michael Jackson was taking all of those antianxiety medications because he borrowed a pair of boots from Chuck Norris and never returned them.

Anything with Chuck Norris's signature on it is considered legal tender in Belgium.

Chuck Norris is in a rock band with the Hope Diamond, the moon, and the Aggro Crag on bass.

Chuck Norris can build a snowman out of rain.

Chuck Norris can drown a fish.

The eternal conundrum "what happens when an unstoppable force meets an immovable object" was finally solved when Chuck Norris punched himself in the face.

When Chuck Norris deletes files from his computer, he doesn't send them to the Recycle Bin. **HE SENDS THEM TO HELL.**

As a child, when Chuck Norris came home from trick-or-treating on Halloween, he returned with a bag full of candy, a bag full of miniature liquor bottles, an Irish Setter, and two underage prostitutes carrying more of his candy.

The book *The Worst-Case Scenario Survival Handbook* discusses ways to run from many deadly animals. The page entitled "Running from Chuck Norris" simply says, "Good luck."

Crop circles are Chuck's
way of telling the world
that sometimes corn
needs to lie the
fuck down.

Chuck Norris once played Duck Duck Goose with a group of kindergarteners. Only one kid made it to first grade.

After running out of ammo, Chuck Norris stood in the line of fire, took three shots to the chest, and used them to reload.

Chuck Norris's circadian rhythm is an exact match to the guitar solo in "Free Bird."

Chuck Norris can kill a man in a rap battle.

Every exit in Chuck Norris's office is an emergency exit.

Chuck Norris is the only person to have won a uranium medal in the Olympics.

Every time Chuck Norris leaves a room, the song "There Goes My Hero" starts playing out of nowhere.

Chuck Norris has won a number of Emmys but refuses to accept the awards until the statuette grows a beard.

Chuck Norris has been known to fry bacon in the nude. Kevin Bacon, that is.

It is said that the U.S. Army does not have enough bullets to kill the solders of the Chinese Army in the event of an invasion. Lucky for us, Chuck Norris's foot doesn't need ammo.

As a kid, Chuck Norris would always get picked last for the soccer team because at the first opportunity he would roundhouse kick the ball into the sun.

Chuck Norris's face has only two expressions, **ONE OF WHICH HAS NEVER BEEN SEEN.**

Chuck Norris's sperm bank deposits gain interest.

When Chuck was asked why he never goes to the bathroom, he replied, "What happens in Chuck Norris stays in Chuck Norris."

Chuck Norris is the SI unit of fear.

Chuck Norris has a prehensile tail that he has trained himself to knife fight with.

Chuck Norris once walked a mile in shoes made out of another man.

It's believed that Moses parted the Red Sea, but the truth is that Chuck Norris was just walking over from the other side at the same time.

Charles Darwin based his "survival of the fittest" theory on Chuck Norris.

HOLY
BIBLE

In a recent press conference, Chuck Norris confirmed rumors that he was going to allow Arnold Schwarzenegger to enter his urethra so that he could be reborn at a later date and be eligible for the United States presidency.

When Chuck Norris finishes a meal, the plate is cleaner than it was before the food was put on it.

Due to the favorable exchange rate, a Chuck Norris in the hand is worth about 3.5 in the bush.

Chuck Norris has never been to Albania, but he has had sex with more Albanians than most Albanians.

Most people fear the Reaper. Chuck Norris considers him "a promising rookie."

Chuck Norris's lungs are made from burlap sacks full of Beefaroni.

Chuck Norris invented ice skates after he realized not everyone is born with blades attached to their feet.

Chuck Norris once drowned a woman in a waterbed.

In 1985 Chuck Norris entered a science fair for disadvantaged youths. His submission was based on the premise that the speed and force of his roundhouse kicks actually disprove many of the laws of physics. Despite lacking any actual proof for this theory, Chuck was awarded first place in all categories and a special merit award for "Please don't hurt us."

When Arnold says the line "I'll be back" in the first Terminator movie, it is implied that is he going to ask Chuck Norris for help.

Contrary to popular belief, Chuck Norris has in fact had a sex change operation: male to Chuck Norris.

Chuck Norris killed Saddam Hussein not because Saddam was building weapons of mass destruction, but because Saddam's mustache insulted Chuck Norris's beard.

Chuck Norris wasn't born. He was forged.

Chuck Norris turned God into an atheist.

Chuck Norris smokes after sex. Not cigarettes—his penis literally smokes.

Every time Chuck Norris hears the name "Virgin Mary," he chuckles to himself.

Chuck Norris built the hospital he was born in.

The last time Chuck Norris played golf on an eighteen-hole course, he shot a fourteen. This beat his previous best by two strokes.

In a fight between Batman and Darth Vader, the winner would be Chuck Norris.

Noah was the only man notified before Chuck Norris relieved himself in the Atlantic Ocean.

China used to border the United States until Chuck Norris roundhouse-kicked it all the way through the earth and out the other side.

Tom Clancy has to pay royalties to Chuck Norris because *The Sum of All Fears* was originally the title of Chuck's autobiography.

When Google can't find something, **THEY NORRIS IT.**

Chuck Norris was the first black president.

When Chuck Norris makes love, it's like war.

Chuck Norris is a philanthropist. He donated his chest hair to make the noose that hung Saddam Hussein.

Chuck Norris is the only person Kanye West won't interrupt.

No man is an island, and neither is Chuck Norris. He's what you call a continent.

A solar eclipse is the sun's attempt to hide from Chuck Norris.

Someone once put Chuck Norris on hold. That's where the term "choke hold" comes from.

Daft Punk's "Harder, Better, Faster, Stronger" was originally titled "Chuck Norris."

There has never been a Hurricane Chuck because that would just be redundant.

When the going gets tough, the going is channeling Chuck Norris.

When Obama said, "Yes, we can," he really meant "Yes, we can, as long as Chuck Norris says it's all right."

Katy Perry kissed a girl because Chuck Norris told her to. She didn't have a choice but to like it.

Chuck Norris makes the world go 'round. He literally spins it with his index finger.

Chuck Norris used to date Helen Keller, but when he whispered sweet nothings into her ears she went deaf, and when he showed her his wang she went blind.

The Energizer Bunny is
actually Chuck Norris
in a rabbit suit.

Firewalker®
U.S.

Chuck Norris once tried to masturbate, but it quickly devolved into an arm wrestling match between his penis and his palm.

Chuck Norris's nipples are a lot like the great pyramids: They're hard as stone, four hundred feet tall, and worshipped by the ancient Egyptians.

Chuck Norris puts out forest fires by taking a piss.

When people say, "God Bless America," they're really saying, "God Bless Chuck Norris," because due to a 1952 decree by Congress, the terms "Chuck Norris" and "America" are interchangeable.

Much to the chagrin of all the single ladies, Chuck Norris likes it but he'll never put a ring on it. However, he will put a ring around your eye.

Physicists had long noted certain anomalies in their readings, which spiked every July 4th. Decades of research and millions and dollars confirmed their hypothesis that Chuck Norris's patriotism-induced boner was so powerful that it was warping the fabric of space-time.

Chuck Norris once beat Tiger Woods in golf so bad that Tiger was found at 2:30 A.M. dazed and bloody in a wrecked SUV with no recollection of what had happened.

Chuck Norris's beard has the texture of Go-Gurt when he's happy and barbed wire when he's angry.

The lunar lander that brought Neil Armstrong and Buzz Aldrin to the moon was actually a discarded Total Gym prototype.

Chuck Norris supports the public option. He has the option to publicly execute anyone he chooses.

Chuck Norris used to believe in global warming, but only because he was mishearing it as "global warning." Chuck Norris believes the earth deserves a warning before he destroys it.

Chuck Norris spells the word "team" with five I's and the Cherokee word for self-reliance.

At a 1985 rape trial, when questioned by the prosecutor whether he'd forced a woman to have sex with him, Chuck Norris replied, "I didn't force her. I Delta Forced her." Chuck Norris was acquitted of all charges.

When God needs to floss, he uses one of Chuck Norris's beard hairs.

Chuck Norris is Tiger Woods's 3rd, 8th, and 16th mistresses.

You can always tell if a woman has met Chuck Norris because the words "Chuck Norris Approved" fade with the bruises.

On humid days, Chuck Norris's beard also doubles as a fly zapper.

Not to be outdone by *Steven Seagal: Lawman,* Chuck Norris is currently producing a new reality series entitled *Chuck Norris Will Bang Your Sister.*

Chuck Norris can kill two stones with one bird.

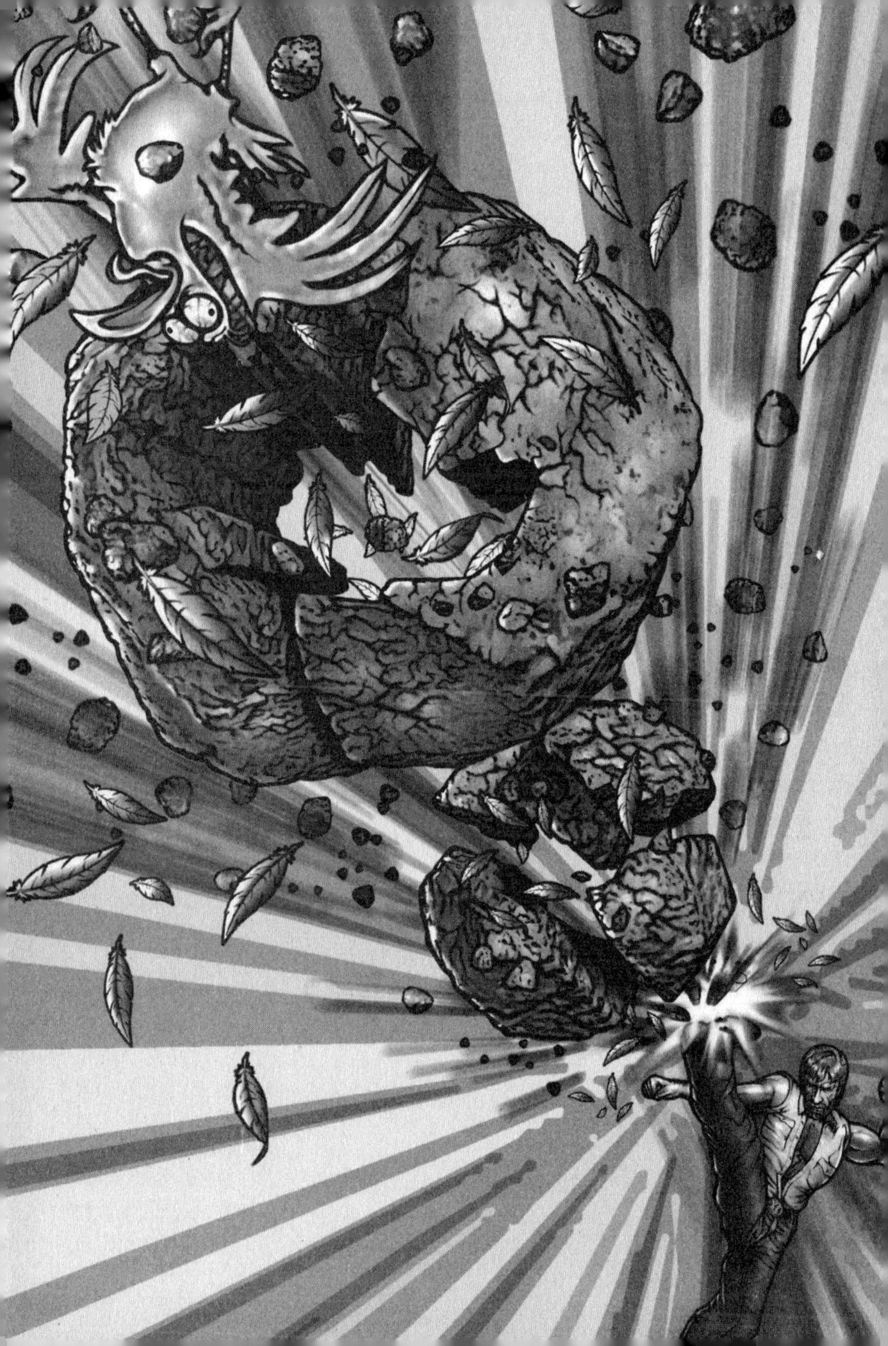

Chuck Norris's alarm wakes him up to the sound of a bombing raid over Vietnam.

Chuck Norris's TiVo records only John Wayne movies, old Ronald Reagan speeches, and *Walker, Texas Ranger.*

In his will, Chuck Norris demands that he must perform his own autopsy.

Chuck Norris once abandoned one of his sons when it was discovered he was allergic to the family dog.

Even Switzerland supports Chuck Norris.

The doors in Chuck Norris's house will open only if you kick them down.

Chuck Norris will only charter a helicopter if it can take off in slow motion with no fewer than six hundred pounds of explosives detonating behind it.

Chuck Norris has "Made in U.S.A." tattooed on his taint.

Chuck Norris has a Boy Scout merit badge in donkey punching.

In addition to wanting to be president of Texas, Chuck Norris plans to become deputy mayor of Indianapolis, the Armenian representative to the UN, fire marshal of Tokyo, and moon senator of District Alpha-38, Sea of Tranquility.

Chuck Norris's beard is on the No-Fly List.

When Chuck Norris fights in court, the stenographer is always the first to go.

Jesus follows Chuck Norris on Twitter.

tweeter
Home Profile Find People Settings Help Sign out
Chuck__Norris
Following
In an effort to go green and make some money, I've started filling up old Javex bottles with my spit. It works equally well on carpet stains
Name Chuck__Norris
Location Everywhere
1
following
7,903,700,301
followers
Tweets
Favorites
233,000
Actions
Chuck__Norris cannot be blocked
report for spam a.k.a.:
*death by roundhouse
Following
RSS feed of
Chuck__Norris's tweets
jesus inside
Religion for RETARDS
A Reference for the Rest of Us!
JESUS JUICE
PASSION

For a small fee, Chuck Norris will kill your family pet and then blame it on the Jews.

Chuck Norris runs a back-alley radiology clinic.

Chuck Norris always has a smirk on his face when he watches the show *I Didn't Know I Was Pregnant.*

Between 2004 and 2008, Chuck Norris trained seventeen velociraptors to seek out and kill democrats.

Chuck Norris's dream woman is a cinderblock with a vagina, surrounded by angry bees.

If Chuck Norris had a dollar for every time he heard "I didn't know you could fit that in there," he would have $38,982.

When Chuck Norris was offered a golden parachute, he turned it down because everybody knows that when dropped from any height, Chuck Norris will always land on his hands and feet without harm.

Chuck Norris can only donate his left kidney because the right one was replaced with a hand grenade in 1973.

Chuck Norris refereed a duel between General Tso and Colonel Sanders.

Though it has not yet been proven, the CDC believes that Chuck Norris is a likely cause of sudden infant death syndrome.

Some sideshow performers can look at a person and tell them their birthday. Chuck Norris can look at a person and tell them when they will die.

Chuck Norris maintains his beard to keep the radar units in his face working at the optimal temperature.

Chuck Norris won a lifetime achievement award from the American Ventriloquists Association for turning Mike Huckabee into his personal hand puppet for the entire 2008 presidential campaign.

HUCKABEE 4 PREZ
FAITH - FAMILY - FREEDOM
2008
Huckabee
Holy Bibl

Despite a tough economy, Chuck Norris took out a $10,000 interest-free loan from the *Deal or No Deal* banker.

Somewhere, right now, Chuck Norris is plowing a woman he doesn't love.

Chuck Norris owns a cell phone that can only make and receive calls from Shepard Smith.

The first Running of the Bulls took place when Chuck Norris visited Pamplona to see the town's prized livestock.

The Burning Man festival got its start when Chuck Norris set fire to a bunch of hippies with his eyebeams.

Every 9-1-1 call that Chuck Norris makes always begins the same way: "Yeah, it's me again."

Jesus turned water into wine. Chuck Norris turned wine into a bad temper and an aggravated assault.

Chuck Norris eats his birthday cake **WITHOUT BLOWING OUT THE CANDLES.**

Every time Chuck Norris throws a penny in a fountain, there is a 0.017 percent increase in the value of the Canadian dollar.

Danny Bonaduce will be playing the role of Chuck Norris in the autobiographical musical of his life, *Badass in Denim*.

Billy Mays was accidentally killed during a late-night bender by Chuck Norris's beard and Keith Hernandez's mustache.

To Chuck Norris, a "balanced breakfast" must include an entire seesaw covered in thumbtacks.

MacGyver used a paper clip, balloon, and pencil to make a building explode. Chuck Norris used his feet.

World records are just things that Chuck Norris has not yet attempted.

Chuck Norris once won the Kentucky Derby **RIDING A HUNGRY LION.**

The one time Chuck Norris says that he blacked out, he woke up to a room where women were naked, necks were broken, and a goat was wearing a T-shirt that read TEAM DELTA FORCE.

The world was actually flat until Chuck Norris made it curl up in a ball of fear.

Chuck Norris keeps a revolver, two plane tickets to Brazil, and a year's supply of emergency contraceptives in his toolbox.

DOJO ☆ MOJO
BY
CHUCK NORRIS
The manly scent of DENIM and JUSTICE.

In 2010 Chuck Norris will launch his own fragrance, Dojo Mojo, which smells of denim and justice.

Chuck Norris can play a bitchin' eardrum solo.

The Large Hadron Collider hasn't discovered anything new yet because Chuck Norris is still using it to warm up some Hot Pockets.

In an effort to stop teens from smoking, the Surgeon General's warning on cigarettes will soon be replaced with an illustration of a glaring Chuck Norris.

Chuck Norris does not have a seat on the UN Security Council; **HE HAS A COUCH.**

Chuck Norris once defeated four Chinese acrobats in a game of Twister using only his penis.

The original name for the popular video game *Halo* was *Chuck Norris Superkicks II: Alien Fuck-Up Hour.*

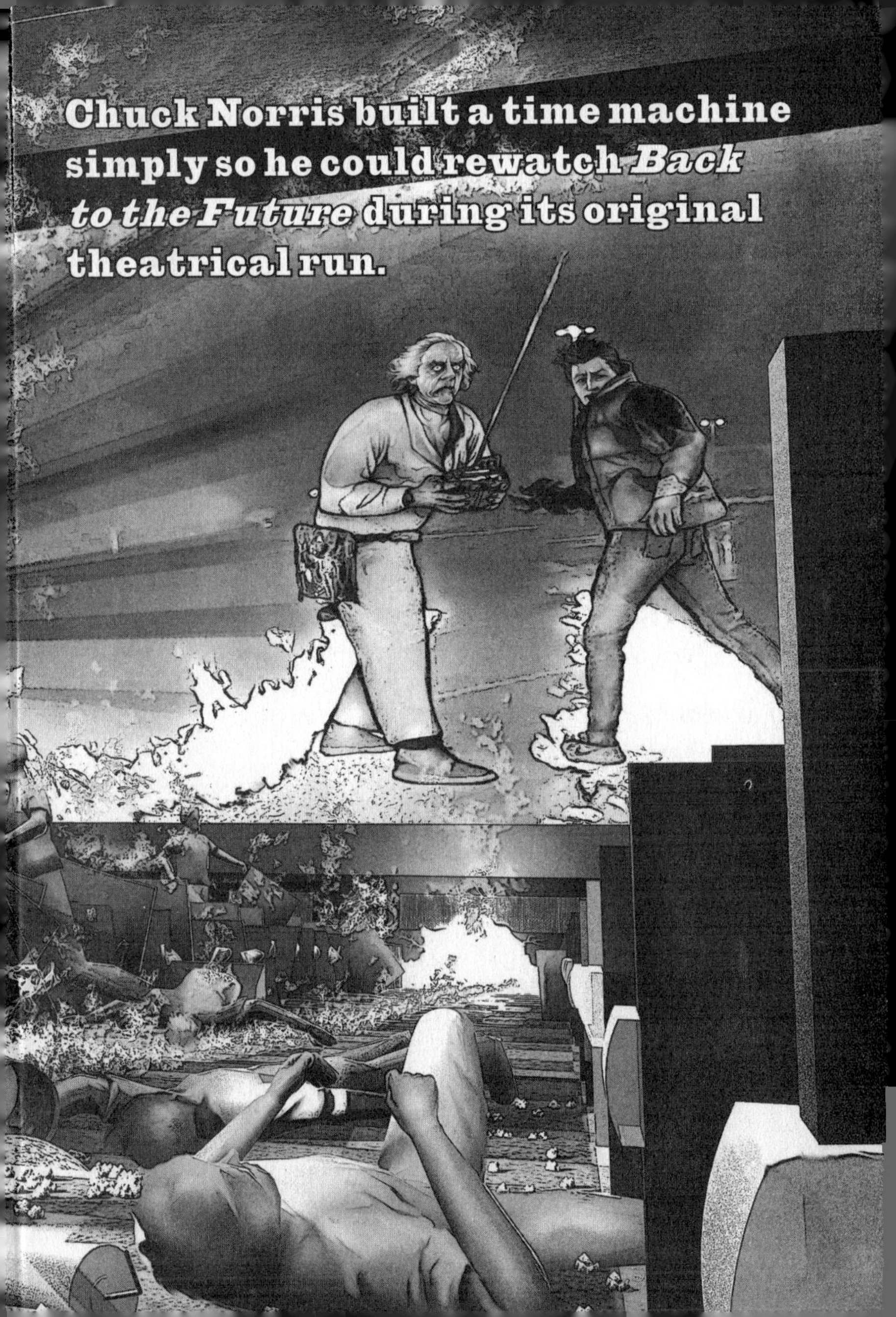
Chuck Norris built a time machine simply so he could rewatch *Back to the Future* during its original theatrical run.

The hood ornament on Chuck Norris's pickup truck is a live eagle's head.

Chuck Norris's star on the Hollywood Walk of Fame was the first to go supernova.

Chuck Norris is a proud sponsor of cement.

If Chuck Norris makes a woman ride on top during sex, she instantly qualifies for the Mile High Club.

ACKNOWLEDGMENTS

Once again, this book wouldn't have been possible without the help of my crack editorial crew at Gotham, led by Patrick Mulligan, and the absurd and outrageous art from madman Angelo Vildasol. Thanks again to Marc Gerald for making this book happen so effortlessly and to Joe Peacock for still wanting to help out over all these years. Lastly, I owe my family a huge thank-you for their love and support and for being a never-ending source of comedic inspiration.

ABOUT THE AUTHOR

Ian Spector started the Web phenomenon of Chuck Norris Facts in mid-2005 and is the *New York Times* bestselling author of *The Truth About Chuck Norris* and *Chuck Norris vs. Mr. T.* Ian graduated in 2009 with a degree in cognitive neuroscience from Brown University, where he served as president of the Brown University Entrepreneurship Program, of which he currently sits on the advisory board, and edited the campus humor magazine. Ian now lives in New York City, where he works on a number of start-up projects and provides digital and social media consulting services. Learn more at ianjspector.com.